A MEASURED UNIVERSE

A MEASURED UNIVERSE

Poetry

GRACE PELLEY

South Eighth & Wyanoke Books

Contents

For Pastor Marvin

Cacophony

In the multitude of voices which I am to celebrate little wisdom can be found.

We seek solutions to complex problems and assume
Since our ancestors could not fix them, the answers must be extraordinarily
Complicated. We scoff at simple answers, calling them idealistic platitudes.
All this is hard, exhausting work, for which we pride
Ourselves. No other people have slaved
So much for equality; we must be the most woke of all.

And yet we wonder how hate still exists. Do not point to sin. An old solution will not satisfy.

In the cacophony of voices little wisdom can be found.

Love is often a quiet thing, a study in nuance
As well as passion. Love is often a simple
Thing, its expressions as common as blue in the sky. Love
Is often a small thing, the recognition of which does not require knowledge.

But come now and be enlightened:
The world is too loud for such a weak
Thing as love. Only a child, or Jesus, would be foolish
Enough to give it power.

September

Nine days after my reluctant request,
I find myself waiting for a friend
Who will take me to what I fear
For a reason I do not know.
When he comes, I speak filled with doubt,
Thinking what I seek belongs to another.
But he quiets me, saying that this is mine.

When he has called our pastor, we come to the place decided,
And I, for fear of presumption, ask if I may kneel,
Humble, abandon myself.
For what is mere man, a child of man
To not kneel in the presence of the Other?

Our pastor asks if I want to pray,
But what can I say?
What new petition could I bring?
If God has me before, I needn't speak now.

And so they pray for me
With words too honorable for me.
They praise virtues I knew not
I possessed.
And fear again steals into me
That they have forgotten why
I have asked for this. For words
Alone are not what I crave
But a sign.
A sign prescribed long before
That I would not have chosen
But has been provided for me:

An anointing with oil,
A blessing for the sick,
The weak, the frail,
And I am sick,
And I am weak,
And I am frail,
In need of grace
Poured out.

But they have not forgotten
And my pastor with the tenderness
That is in our Lord
Takes oil,
Pours it onto his fingers
And places it upon
My head and soul
In a cross.
For when Jesus had healed the sick
He healed the soul with blood,
His blood,
Grace poured out.
Poured out to call me
Beautiful,
Beloved,
His.

I am bought with blood
As a sign of love,
Love poured out.

Bodies

Was God thinking of me
When He made
The cerebrum?
Did He weep
Knowing that I would fight
Against the constraints
A little misplaced
Blood would lay on me?
     He made it anyway.

When Jesus created wrists,
Ankles and heads;
When He decided
The consequences of piercing
Skin; when He decreed
All the ways a body would fail,
Did He see His and reserve for Himself
The most heinous death?
     He made Himself a body anyway.

Ordained and Dwindling

This world has nothing
To suggest your absence
Is finite.
Your very existence is acknowledged
In no songs, no stories. We have no hope
Except our Father.

I do not know the number
Of tears I will cry, of days I will live
Until I will hold you. I imagine
The timer marking
Our separation will expire. I hope
For this against all evidence:
The ocean between us appears permanent.

The One Who will bring you to me
Keeps count of the fixed decades and seconds,
Ordained and dwindling,
Until you, my brother, are finally
In my arms.

The World to Come is This One

We will be lifted
Like furniture removed
For a vacuum, taken up
For a moment
And set back
Down for eternity.

This place, this home,
This world, this is the one
That is to come.

Absurd

Once you accept that everything is absurd, a great deal of things begin to make sense. Like how people would give up comfort to proclaim a God they've never seen to people they've never met. Or that people would be thankful for pain. Rationalizing such things always fails. If you try to explain it, you will only gain a headache. You could, of course, simply accept the absurdity of the Cross.

It will cost your life. But, it's not like you were planning to keep it.

After For King & Country's "Shoulders"

It does not happen often.
Something wanders into my small
World. Something that makes sense.
It knows of both gurneys
And anointings.
It sees me completely.

This peculiar scrutiny is the only place
I am not afraid.

Hunger No More

You don't have to go anywhere
Else to be satisfied. He is the Living
Bread. Aren't you tired of sifting
Through the noise? How long will you dine at tables
That serve inadequate
Substitutes? You can walk away
From narratives will never satisfy.

You will be hated
For what you no longer consume, but you will hunger
No more.

Lewis & Tolkien

The professors talk about death.

The first thinks it is rest.
When the heaviness of loss
Will not relent, and the only companions
We want are gone,
Another land with greener hills
Sweeps into view. We cannot fight
Here anymore.

The second has another view: death is the beginning
Of the greatest adventure.
We do not yet know the stories
That will unfold. Death is the threshold
Between good and great. We can charge into death
Knowing it will send
Us to life.

The difference is a matter of time.

Macadamia

Pastor's class again had a teacher.

She wanted to know our birthdays
And our favorite cookies. "White chocolate macadamia nut,"
I volunteered, thinking it a very sophisticated
Cookie for an eleven-year-old
To like.

After all I knew
The word "autopsy."
I wanted to know what the grown-ups
Were saying and their answers
To our questions:
Why did Pastor die?
Would the church stay open?
Who would take the church?
And the question no one asked
But I longed to have answered:
Who would take care of me?

The new pastor had many plans
For the church, but they didn't include
Me. He put off baptizing
My sisters and me. We privileged
Kids were too stable
For his attention.

I'd asked Pastor to baptize me, but he forgot.

I was seventeen
Before I threw up my hands,

Begging another:
"Please,
Please be my pastor.
Please take care
Of me." But before that, I had others who tried,
Even when I did not see it, to help me,
Starting with the teacher from the suburbs
And her macadamia cookies.

Secure

Beyond what we can see is the real
Reality and its good, gracious King. He exalts children
And crowns those the world discards. Already His rule
Is slipping out from the veil and finding us. The curtain
Will be lifted soon, and we'll know
He never could have lost.

There is nothing to fear.

The Field of May

This distant shore that cradles us
We cannot call home.
And though this place succors us,
Still we long to roam.
So, we wish not to stay
    And soon we will be on our way
    Away, away
    To the Field of May.

When Heaven and Earth mingle
And we join the merry thong,
Jerusalem, the crowning jewel,
But to dwell there would be wrong.
Home is where we wish to stay;
    O, let us be away
    Away, away
    To the Field of May.

Gurney

I thought He would be in the medicine
Coursing up my back to my hands. He was not.

Where was God on the day we discovered Baclofen
Was not the answer, two days before we learned there is no answer?

He was where He had to be.
On the gurney, next to me.

Preview

I watch as you cut
Dead skin off my feet.
Perhaps the other patients don't watch, but it brings my remedy:
What is removed can no longer hurt me.

We talk about the things of God. A sweetness
Foreign to many fills
The treatment room. You understand my callous
And my soul.
Few see both.

Your office houses a preview
Of my healing: here with my cure
And your gentleness.
The pain leaves for a while
When you have done your work.

It doesn't hurt. It isn't complicated.

It has everything a full, desperate room with would-be healers room lacks.

Easter

I have seen the noblest of men quake
Before me, but they often alone,
And Dietrich is not. Jesus
Is walking him over to me.
I watch him pray in the grey yard from the top
Of the gallows. He isn't trembling
From fear like most people do when I come
For them. No, he is compliant
With his death sentence.
His tremors are only from the cold.

Jesus orders me
Not to let Dietrich linger,
So the rope has only been around his neck
A few seconds when I snatch his soul.

It's not a long journey
Through the thin veil
Between shadow and substance.

After they travel my short
Road, Dietrich in Jesus' arms,
I perch at the edge of Paradise,
Watching Dietrich soak in the sweet, green warmth
Of life itself. I watch Jesus embrace him.

And so life begins.

Heaven's Dominion

My brother has been living in Heaven
These twenty-seven years
In the unmitigated, glorious presence
Of the Ancient of Days.
He is there by the decree
Of our Father
For the praise of His Name.

Son of Man

I have not given my life
Over to an idea, a philosophy
Or to a set of practices, but to a Person,
A Man.

And this Man has claimed
My adoration by giving me Himself.

The Last Sacrament

I have been told sin
Causes death, but I do not yet
Grasp what death is.

Death is the last
Sacrament, the last acting out
Of what we can never fathom:

The Cross.

Liturgy

Welcome, welcome. Jesus
Has brought you here and welcomes
You into His presence.
What we are about to do
Has been done
For two thousand years,
And it will keep you.

When you sing,
You join with a multitude
Around the world
And those who have passed on.
You are singing with your heroes
And your family.
All of them are cheering you on.
Though you cannot see or hear them.
They will keep you.

When you pray,
The Maker of Heaven and Earth,
He Who was and is and is to come, hears
You. He is with you always,
No matter your concern.
He will keep you.

When you hear the Word,
The Spirit comes to you
With its true meaning.
He keeps you from sin
And gives you Himself.
He will keep you.

When you eat and drink,
The crucified body of Jesus
Enters you.
It is your strength against sin
And so many weary days.
It will keep you.

When the world is loud,
When you are betrayed,
When you have sinned,
If the Jesus Whom this liturgy reveals
Enters you heart, then until the day
Your faith becomes sight
We, His Body, will keep you.

Privilege and Cages

You did not make
This for me. You had others
In mind, others with normal
Arms and legs.

Sometimes, with luck and grit
And help, I can use what was not made
For me. You get very excited when I do.
I never mention it was you
Who made it without thinking of me.

You put me on a pedestal for the smallest
Of achievements. It's lonely
Up here. You crown me special,
Different. You admire me too much to let
Me come down. I love you, but I hate
This perch and dream of being unremarkable,
Of belonging.

Tanks

If tanks roll into the Field of May with the Antichrist at their helm,
I will not fear,
For Jesus will comfort me.

If the deception falls thick, and everyone I love turns away,
I will remain faithful,
For Jesus will preserve me.

If I am deprived of a home,
I will watch the skies for my eternal home's descent,
For Jesus will receive me.

But if Jesus leaves my side, I am damned.

The Messiah

Tonight I will sit and listen
To music I cannot make,
Each word reverberating,
Coming as the voice of God
Tuning the sounds of my soul.

I imagine
The Messiah Himself sitting
Among us,
Enthroned and smiling.

Creaturely Reminiscence

I can no longer kneel
At the altar where I was anointed.
The silence waiting to be broken
By words too weighty for me
Seems to linger there. My body remembers
The smooth wood that held me. I miss
That church, its rhythm and its people.
I miss the place
Itself: the morning light
Coming through the windows, the quiet chapel
That witnessed my anointing.

The pastor who anointed me showed
Us that the sanctuary still stands.
Whenever I see it, my mind
Walks up the aisle, turns down the hall and sees
The chapel again. I never
Left it, not all of me.

Trespassers Will Violate

You do not know Whom
You have slandered. You think of power
Without realizing that the strength
To make good from wrong
Is a mighty one. You see a problem
To be fixed; I see an estate
To be stewarded. O fool!
You do not know that you have entered
Into the holy. Your "kindness" is a transgression.

You do not object
To me: this body
Mine is not mine. It belongs
To a Holy God.
He determines the wayward
Path of every neuron. I have signed
Over to Him the disability
That is dissonant to your thinking.

For my healing is being saved
Until my work is fulfilled.
Then shall it be accomplished.
Gentleness will take its place
With power;
A Father's touch;
A Healer's touch;
A Husband's touch;
An intimacy lost
On you. Please, pitiful
Man, do not disturb
What He has planned for me.

A Psalm

The ways of the Lord are good,
Giving life to His servants.
The will of the Lord is pure,
Giving joy to His children.

To suffer with the Lord is an honor,
For He chastens those He loves;
Those He is saving feel pain.
Those He esteems enter this sacred fellowship.

Woe to the one who boasts in his own strength,
Woe to the one who boasts in his heart, "I do not need God."
Such a man will come to ruin;
Those who remember him will fade.

But not so with the righteous.
Those who fear the Lord will endure,
Those who do His bidding will live.
For He will give them life.
In the day of trouble, they will not be disturbed.
Even in the day of death, they will find the strength to praise their God.

In the presence of the Lord is life,
In the will of the Lord is peace.
In the judgments of the Lord I find no fault,
I delight in all His ways.

The Lord is everlasting.
Only by His hand are we saved.
The wicked shall pass away,
But the children of God shall serve Him forever.

God's Priest

He had waited for her. Even before He had surrendered His body to His cousin, He knew she would come.

For Him.

She was His bridge between being laid in water and on wood. Flat on His back. Calloused hands pinning Him down.

We would have sent a priest to Him. Not her, the town harlot.

He had anticipated her all day. She was coming to do for Him what He could not do for Himself.

Though she tried to be silent, He heard her enter. They examined each other. Messiah and prostitute. Savior and sinner. God and His Priest.

She came to Him. God acted upon. He leaned against her. God dependent upon. She anointed Him. God let her.

No wonder we doubted He was God.

The woman we were told to shun anointed Jesus.

It was disgraceful. It was undignified.

It was necessary. It was beautiful.

He lost Himself in the sacred act. "Before You die," it seemed to say, "You need this. Here is Your strength. Before Your Father carries You to death, Your body has been sanctified."

A few days later, He looked down and saw His life ending. He declared victory and lay Himself down in darkness. He was ready because of her.

I too have placed my body in other's hands. I have been lifted on to a table on which I did not want lay and given air I did not want breathe. And I have seen my limits.

I have nothing left to do, no other recourse but this: to prepare for death as He did. To count all my plans flimsy and negotiable. To see no one as unqualified to help me.

I submit to Him to do for me what I cannot do for myself, which is everything. I lay myself in His arms, all my weight upon Him.

Light

The nearness of God brings Light.
Even when children die
Before birth, there is Light.

Before God made the heavens
And the earth, He came close. Before He made
The grass and the animals,
Before He conquered the waters, He drew
Near. Before He made us, He filled the earth with Himself.

The nearness of God is Light.

Rich amid Scarcity

I would not have chosen
A path so barren of friendship.
Others do not wander
This way, beside a damaged cerebrum
And an anointing I will never understand.

My twisted hand did not trace
The limits of my life. But a Scarred One
Did. To dwell in this small
Oasis with Him is better
Than any other place's
Temporal pleasure.

Second Language

We could exist
Without music. Jazz did not
Build the pyramids, and pop
Did not give us science. Yes, we could
Exist without music, but
We could only exist.

What would comfort
Us when words fall short, or breathe for us
When we cannot?
What would steady us?
How would we make sense of the joy
That sweeps over us? How would we dance together?
Where would harmony go?

If we did not have music
We would walk around looking
For something we could not name,
Mourning a loss without definition.

Sabbath

Come out from the night
And into the warmth. Your day has been long.
Sit down for a while, and soon you will see
This big world still spins
Even while you sleep.

You fought all day long
For things you can't earn.
Haven't I told you? But I'll tell you again:
You are not the reason this big world
Still spins. How tired you look, my dear,
How very tired
You are. Why don't you go lie
Down and rest?

I'll rock you while you sleep,
And keep this big world spinning.

You were never meant to do such things.

Joy

He spoke of joy,
And then He died.
I cannot help
But wonder why
We think of joy
With parties and good company.

Here is joy:
You needn't worry about yourself
Ever again.
For when the path is easy
You have Jesus,
And when it is rough
You have Jesus.
And when you die—
And die you must—
You will know
The Christ of the cross
Like never before.

He is joy.

The God Who Stays

Eternal God, I do not know why You have condescended
To dwell with me, or why You take an interest in my existence.
I am a small woman with many needs.
> You stay with me.

My Jesus, You know well the disgraces to which my body subjects me.
> You stay with me.

Holy Spirit, You know how often I wonder if goodness really is rewarded.
> You stay with me.

Triune God who dwells in unapproachable light, this is a great mystery:
> You stay with me.

Let the Parting Not Be Bitter

Let the parting not be bitter
Though our fellowship is sweet.
At the end of this long winter
We in fairer lands shall meet.

Though the path before is dreary
And our hearts give way to fear,
On His breast we will be carried
For the King of Heaven is here!

Press we on the road before us,
Though much smoother ones we've seen,
Press we on the path with Jesus;
On His arm we'll always lean.

Enduring Rest

I have spent two Septembers
In this room, and I cannot fathom a better
Place to be. At first I was incredulous
And tried to earn this gift,
But then I realized that I could not reject
The Giver of beautiful things:
Flowers of favor,
Diamonds of covenant love,
Fine clothes that mark me as His.

This room has a place
For everything: Love, hurt, dreams, sorrow;
They are no longer falling
On top of me. I can walk away from them all
And rest. All I ever wanted was rest.
My Father's voice fills
The room, a song for me, the poured-out-upon one:

Mine!
Mine!
Mine!

A Measured Universe

The women come and go
Talking of Michelangelo
And a poet freshly dead.
We listen to their heads
For a minute or two.
How much they presume.

My work, a bug pinned, open for interpretation
By people who know nothing of my creation;
Collected, explained, and categorized,
Its true meaning creeps about disguised.
They will never discover my intentions
Or how they vomit indiscretions,
Nor do they care for beauty.
They leave believing they have done their duty.

But perhaps, after dinner's last crumbs have been swept
And all the mourners have prudently wept,
A woman of no consequence will return home
And drown out the day with her favorite tome.
There she will find a phrase that stirs her brain
And reminds her of something she cannot explain,
But which I called September.
The pinpricks of light
In the not-quite-night
Help her remember:

The universe is not to be apprehended, quantified or collected
But appreciated, loved, and revered, for in it glory is reflected,
Just like the people in this small place
With whom we journey as we are propelled through space.

Acknowledgements

Thank you to Dr. Kristy Ingram, who provided editorial feedback.

About the Author

Grace Pelley is a freelance writer and a contributor to The Mighty. She helps Christian women write novels through editing, emotional support and project management so that they can give hope to others through their stories. Learn more at SecondChanceBookCoaching.com.

CPSIA information can be obtained
at www.ICGtesting.com
Printed in the USA
BVHW012115030622
638873BV00004B/73